An Hachette UK Company
www.hachette.co.uk

First published in Great Britain in 2013 by
Spruce, a division of Octopus Publishing Group Ltd
Endeavour House
189 Shaftesbury Avenue
London
WC2H 8JY
www.octopusbooks.co.uk
www.octopusbooksusa.com

Distributed in the US by
Hachette Book Group USA
237 Park Avenue
New York NY 10017 USA

Distributed in Canada by
Canadian Manda Group
165 Dufferin Street
Toronto, Ontario, Canada M6K 3H6

Trevor Davies asserts the moral right to be identified as the author of this work

ISBN 978-1-84601-424-6

A CIP catalogue record for this book is available from the British Library

Printed and bound in China

2 4 6 8 10 9 7 5 3 1

PUPPIES

FOR WHEN SH*T HAPPENS...

spruce

Trevor Davies

CONTENTS

INTRODUCTION

What do you do when faced with a puppy? Run? Fight? Bark wildly? Or do you forget all your troubles and talk to it like it's a baby? I sense it's the latter. The soothing effect of young canines is so strong that the Red Cross always carry a Beagle and two Shih Tzus when they enter a war zone. And it's why I've created this book of emergency puppies for everyday problems. It's less a book, more a crisis survival manual.

How to use this book
1. Locate your specific emergency on the contents page.
2. Turn the pages until you find the appropriate puppy.
3. Feel your troubles disappear*.

It's important to stress that the emergencies that we've trained our puppies to relieve are more the emotional than the physical kind: affairs of the heart or work-related stress, for example. If you've picked up this book because you ve fallen down a well (a situation that dogs have a good track record of sorting out) or you re simply in the early stages of a heart attack, I urge you to take a moment and consider whether putting this book down and phoning the relevant emergency service might be more prudent. There s only so much a puppy can do. However, if you ve just split up from a partner, or are feeling physically inadequate, then you re in the right place.

Disclaimers

Should you read this book and still feel stressed, consult your doctor, therapist or bookstore (it could be that you re in need of a kitten rather than a puppy, in which case you need *Kittens For When Sh*t Happens*, conveniently published by the same people).

Lastly, very few puppies were badly harmed in the making of this book. Probably no more than 20 or so.

*Adult dosage – no more than two puppies a day, after meals. Store out of reach of children and always read the collar.

Home
emergencies

Sunday afternoon + 90 degrees in the shade + three beers = Fuck mowing the lawn.

Bored with chores?

Moving home?

Garden looks awful?

Herbie regretted scoffing the chocolate and pistachios as it was going to make baking the chocolate and pistachio brownies a tad tricky.

Culinary failure?

As far as Baldwin was concerned, Edmund had gone too far in asserting that Scooby-Doo was a humanist reactionary responding to the latent christianity of Sport Goofy. He could ruddy well talk to the paw!

Annoying housemate?

After his third attempt, Cecil finally decided to get a plumber in.

DIY disaster?

Broken something?

Doug had enjoyed burying Doug Jnr in the sand, but now he realized that he might have been a bit over-zealous. He wasn't even sure that this was the right beach.

Lost something valuable?

Day-to-day travails

Bad hair day?

Bismarck just wished that Gizmo would fuck off and get his own piña colada.

Desperate for a drink?

Within three hours Mr Party would become Mr Crying-Over-the-Toilet-Bowl.

Hungover?

He knew it was wrong, but he couldn't help logging on to leghumpers.com.

Feel guilty?

Fashion disaster?

Weather woes?

Why did I do that?

Road rage?

Although Penelope was on a diet, she couldn't live without her post-dinner sausage.

No self-control?

It was no good. How could she sleep knowing that she'd let the postman off scot-free this morning?

Insomnia?

Can't get out of bed?

Morgan and Meatloaf offered the vet their usual salute.

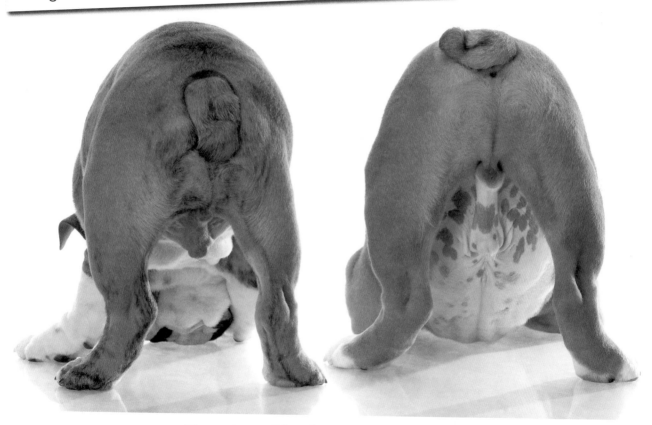

Got out of bed the wrong side?

Angus died fat but happy after eating twice his own body weight in kibble.

Over-indulged?

Been caught out?

Roger suddenly realized that he probably shouldn't have let the handbrake off without checking he could reach the pedals.

Wish you hadn't started something?

Just can't help yourself?

Barney's trip to the Natural History Museum had been a resounding success.

Done something you shouldn't have?

It was Bubble's first time on jury service and she was determined to make an impression.

Trying too hard?

Made a bad call?

Hunter's first attempt at text sex had been going really well until the predictive function turned his sentence into 'I want to sniff your butter.'

Technophobic?

This time he was facing a long stretch. He'd been caught peddling out-of-date liver sausage in a 'borrowed' collar.

11 09 94
L A M B O

Landed yourself in trouble?

The genie had only granted him one wish and Harold now regretted choosing flight over longer legs.

Living with regrets?

Work
worries

Maxwell's new boss told Maxwell to look him in the eye and tell him he'd lost the contract.

Boss hates you?

If Comet was going to be a fighter pilot he needed to feel like one.

Unfair expectations?

The director of the commercial was getting a little fed up with Buster's lack of cute compliance.

Stuck in a dead-end job?

Dealing with idiots?

Neville's plans for world domination were on hold for 20 minutes.

Lacking motivation?

Need a pay rise?

Alf was looking forward to his first day's work at the undertakers.

In the wrong job?

Rocco s checklist:

- ✗ Double espresso
- ✗ Dig up flower bed
- ✗ Bark at neighbours
- ✗ Pogo
- ✗ Tear Emmy's teddy to pieces
- ✗ Pee on garden ornaments
- ✗ Run around in circles
- ✗ Sleep on ironing

Too much coffee?

Colin refused to use his special powers for good or evil, just for chasing tennis balls.

Failing to live up to your potential?

As his turn came nearer, Stanley began having doubts that bull-fighting was for him.

Out of your depth?

Relationship
problems

Harvey's date was going swimmingly and she was very accommodating. It was only when he took her back to his basket that things began to unravel.

Constant failure?

Malcolm thought he'd faced it all: bankruptcy, sex addiction, divorce, bladder infection. But now his kids wanted a DNA test.

Nervous breakdown?

This was the last time Clifford would take up Dillon's invitation to pull his finger.

Tiresome companion?

It wouldn't be long before Tim's Internet history caused cracks in his marriage.

Rocky relationship?

Suspect infidelity?

For Wilson it was true love, for Snowdrop it was purely sexual.

Taken for granted?

Was this real affection or did Rowena have some chicken stuck between her teeth?

62   Worried about your marriage?

Always pick the wrong person?

Unwanted attention?

He knew it wasn't Christmas, but Bazooka wasn't going to give up.

Persistent offender?

By morning Miffy would be gone, along with Frank's wallet and his dignity.

Misread a situation?

This wasn't the right time to tell Brooke that last week's visit to the vet had left Ralph less of a dog than he'd been before.

Don't want to tell your partner? 67

Unlucky in love?

Why, on this day of all days, did her mind drift towards Tiber, the dashing Doberman from Accounts?

Cold feet?

Feeling lonely?

Even Pickwick had to admit that, as knock-backs go, the restraining order was a bit of a blow.

Still hold a candle?

Badger realized he was going to need a hat if he wanted to fit in with the West Coast Santa Posse.

Feel like you don't belong?

Desperate for love?

Family
frustrations

Ziggy and I have been chatting and we've decided to tell you about the car… oh, and the cigarettes. Oh, and Ziggy's tattoo – it's quite tasteful.

Naughty children?

Not only was Peanut's toothache bringing her down, but she couldn't tell her husband that the bandage was too tight.

Annoying partner?

So it wasn't a diamanté collar, it was another fucking bone.

Disappointing present?

Titan's attempt to avoid trick-or-treaters took an unfortunate turn when she chose the worst hiding place possible.

Seasonal stress?

Diesel couldn't bring himself to tell the others what he'd seen floating out there, but there was no way he was going back in the water.

Bad holiday?

Feel unappreciated?

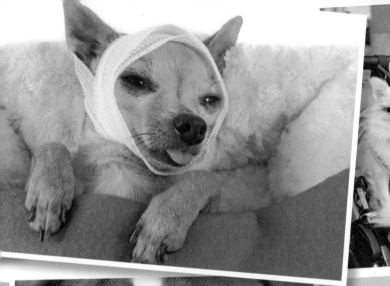

Age, health
and hope

Waffle was determined to make an impression on his first date.

Confidence issues?

Feel old?

Beatrice was hoping that she'd make less of an impact on bigger scales.

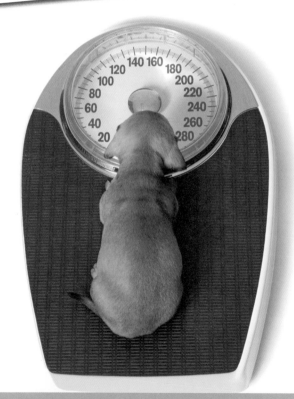

Worried about your weight?

Had your hopes dashed?

In an effort to lose a few pounds Maude had decided to skip dessert.

Can't keep the weight off?

Tyson's diet had been an incredible success, but he couldn't help thinking that chocolate tastes better than skinny feels.

Diet depression?

His team had lost again and Derek needed a hug… from anyone.

Sports failure?

Image problems?

Agnes had found the perfect solution to everyone staring at her big ears.

Self-conscious?

Although the face pack had taken years off her, Clarice was still determined to go ahead with the breast augmentation.

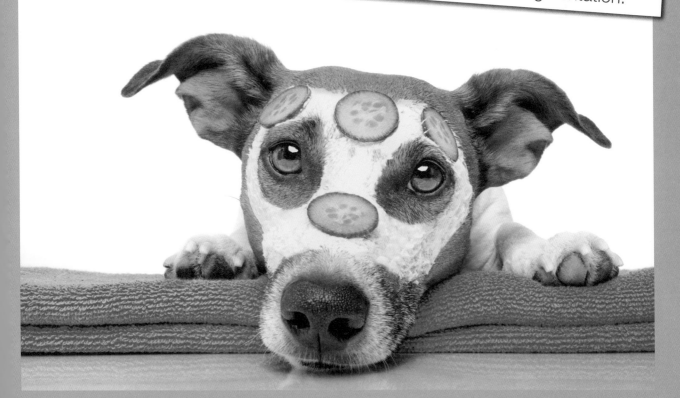

Hate the way you look?

Every day that Kenneth spent with his genitals intact was another day listening out for the words 'vet visit'.

Paranoid?

With glasses from Gucci, fur by Giovanni and perfume by Princess Pooch, the Stiletto Sisters were hitting the town.

Obsessed with your appearance?

ACKNOWLEDGEMENTS

Picture credits

age footstock/Arco/C Steimer 33; Darwin Wiggett 51; Gerard Lacz 84; John McAllister 31; Juniors Bildarchiv GmbH 56; RF Company 61; Sherry Lemcke 42 below right, 45. **Alamy**/8 below right; Andreas Altenburger 83 above right, 95; Annette Shaff 69, 83 above left, 91; Balfour Studios 37; blickwinkel/Schmidt-Roeger 55 above right, 68; Corbis Premium RF 11; Igorr Norman 19 above right, 30; Juniors Bildarchiv GmbH 8 below left, 9 above right, 14, 17, 28, 38, 63, 74 above left, 75 above right, 77, 90; Petra Wegner 54 above right, 64; Photo Network 34; SuperStock 13, 59; Tim James/The Gray Gallery 41; Tomii, Yoshio/SuperStock 9 above left; Wildlife GmbH 8 above left, 10 42 below left, 48, 54 below left, 67. **Ardea**/John Daniels 72. **Corbis**/Chris Carroll 1, 39; Dale Spartas 47; Erik Isakson 86; Ocean 82 below left, 88; Tobi Seftel 40; Ursula Klawitter 74 below right, 78. **Fotolia**/Antonio Gravante 43 above right, 52; Barbara Helgason 94; Javier Brosch 82 above left, 93; Nataliya Kuznetsova 54 below right, 62; Willee Cole 3, 32. **Getty Images**/Allison Michael Orenstein 57; Andrew Bret Wallis 55 above left, 60; Andrew Gowen 19 below left, 27, Beate Zoellner 18 below left, 25; Brand New Images 65; Dan Hallman 43 below left, 50; G. K. Hart/Vikki Hart 18 above right, 22; Lambert 75 above left, 81; Life On White 18 above left, 20; Mark Kolbe 8 above right, 12; Martin Poole 16, 35, 36; Matthew Burditt Photography 6, 9 below left, 15; Reggie Casagrande 54 above left, 70; Retales Botijero 24, 82 below right, 92; Sharon Montrose 55 below left, 58; Steven Puetzer 82 above right, 87; Susan Werner 75 below left, 79; Teresa Guerrero 74 above right, 80; Vanilla Monkey Bear 29; Virginia Macdonald Photographer In 83 below left, 85. **Glow Images**/Gerard Lacz 19 above left; Gerard Lacz/AAI 21; SuperStock 89. **Nature Picture Library**/Adriano Bacchella 73. **Photoshot**/B. Schmid/Clover 42 above left, 53; Mark Taylor/Bruce Coleman 43 above left, 46, 49. SuperStock 23. **Warren Photographic** 18 below right, 26, 42 above right, 44, 66, 71, 74 below left, 76.

Publisher: Sarah Ford
Managing Editor: Clare Churly
Designer: Eoghan O'Brien
Layouts by Ben Tiller
Picture Library Manager: Jennifer Veall
Assistant Production Manager: Lucy Carter